Spreading the Word Further

Spreading the Word Further

Guidelines for Disseminating Development Research

Julie Fisher, Frank Odhiambo and Andrew Cotton

Water, Engineering and Development Centre
Loughborough University
2003

Water, Engineering and Development Centre,
Loughborough University,
Leicestershire, LE11 3TU, UK

© WEDC, Loughborough University, 2003

ISBN 13 Paperback: 978 1 84380 047 7
ISBN Ebook: 9781788533560
Book DOI: http://dx.doi.org/10.3362/9781788533560

A catalogue record for this book is available from the British Library.

A reference copy of this publication is also available online at:
http://www.lboro.ac.uk/wedc/publications/

Fisher, J., Odhiambo, F. O. and Cotton, A. P. (2003)
Spreading the Word Further:
Guidelines for Disseminating Development Research

WEDC (The Water, Engineering and Development Centre) at Loughborough University
in the UK is one of the world's leading institutions concerned with education, training,
research and consultancy for the planning, provision and management of physical
infrastructure for development in low- and middleincome countries.

This edition is reprinted and distributed by Practical Action Publishing.
Since 1974, Practical Action Publishing has published and disseminated books and
information in support of international development work throughout the world.
Practical Action Publishing trades only in support of its parent charity objectives and an
profits are covenanted back to Practical Action (Charity Reg. No. 247257, Group VAT
Registration No. 880 9924 76).

This document is an output from a project funded by the UK
Department for International Development (DFID)
for the benefit of low-income countries.
The views expressed are not necessarily those of DFID.

Designed at WEDC by Sue Plummer

Acknowledgements

We are indebted to the following people and organisations who made valuable contributions to Phase 2 of this research in a variety of ways, including workshop facilitation, key informant interviewing and data analysis:

Ines Restrepo Tarquino Edgar Quiroga	Instituto de Investigación y Desarrollo en Agua Potable, Saneamiento Básico y Conservación del Recurso Hidrico (CINARA), Cali Colombia.
Bilqis Hoque	Environment and Population Research Centre (EPRC), Dhaka, Bangladesh.
Kerry Harris, Kate Skinner, Jabu Masondo, Carolien van der Voorden	MVULA Trust, Johannesburg, South Africa.

The organisations listed in Table 1 (see pages 38-39) were those from which individuals participated as workshop attendees and interviewees in the course of the research.

List of boxes

List of tables

Contents

Executive summary

The purpose of this project *R7127 Enhancing TDR research: Practical guidance on research dissemination strategies* is to improve the impact of Knowledge and Research (KaR) through identifying and comparing appropriate dissemination strategies. The rationale for this research comes out of the increasing acknowledgement and understanding that has developed in recent years of the importance of getting research findings out to those who stand to benefit from them. This report is aimed at a range of readers, including those commissioned by DFID to carry out research in the water and sanitation sector, although the guidelines should also have relevance to researchers in other development sectors and to those working for other donor organisations. In addition, it should be useful for personnel from local government, NGOs, CBOs and private sector firms who are involved in dissemination of research and DFID personnel with formal responsibility or particular interest in research and dissemination issues.

This project has been a two phase study and this book refers to phase two of the research. The purpose of the second phase was to validate ideas from phase one of the Spreading the Word project with a Southern audience of information users and disseminators. A raft of mainly qualitative methodological techniques was employed to fulfil the purpose of this second phase.

Five key critical themes with associated lessons learned resulted from the data analysis. From these, a set of preliminary guidelines have been suggested with checklist points to aid implementation. The five key areas identified are:

1. The importance of planning and implementing a strategic, organisational dissemination strategy where possible, combining the experience of all key players at institutional, project and field level.

2. As part of developing such a strategy, the need to know about our intended audiences through an assessment of user information needs, demand for and relevance of the project findings, and importantly, socio-cultural and resource factors influencing information receipt.

3. Based on what is known about our target audience, it is then possible to target them via appropriate dissemination pathways, providing information which is relevant in terms of content and is presented in accessible formats.

4. Dissemination activity should be financially and practically viable for the chosen period for maximum impact. Suggestions are made of measures which can offset some of the difficulties caused by often inadequate resources (time and personnel).

5. Finally, the importance of monitoring and evaluating the impact of dissemination is reinforced and several examples of methods and indicators are provided, which come directly from the consultation process.

Section 1

Introduction

The purpose of the study

The purpose of this project R7127 *Enhancing TDR research: Practical guidance on research dissemination strategies* is to improve the impact of Knowledge and Research (KaR) through identifying and comparing appropriate dissemination strategies. The *Spreading the Word* research has been about exploring various options for the dissemination of information, in terms of appropriate formats and pathways by which to send information out. Clearly, some researchers may be very familiar with their target audiences and know the best ways to reach them, while others may need guidance on planning a dissemination strategy, what issues to consider and what methods might be effective for particular users.

Why we are doing this work

In recent years, a better acknowledgement and understanding has developed of the importance of getting research findings out to those who stand to benefit from them. This conceptual change has taken place within a wider context than the development sector alone, more especially the health and social policy research disciplines. However, knowledge management within the development sector is a growth area of interest, which has benefited from the studies in other disciplines whilst itself adding significantly to the knowledge base on this topic.

Saywell and Cotton (1999) provide a useful overview of these developments and of the concerns raised by international fora, sector professionals and resource centres in the development arena. Examples that can be cited include the perceived weaknesses in information management identified at the United Nations Conference on Environment and Development (UNCED) and the identified need to improve knowledge sharing. Similarly Chapter 40 of Agenda 21 argues that all stakeholders are information users and providers, reinforcing the need for effective dissemination and knowledge sharing. These concerns have filtered down to key institutions in the international community such as UK

Research Councils and the European Commission, which both require outline strategies for dissemination of project outputs and for user engagement with the project.

Dissemination has been highlighted by the World Bank (1998) for its role in advancing economic and social wellbeing. DFID (1997) (2003) has linked knowledge sharing to achieving its aims of international development and poverty alleviation. Recently, DFID's Target Strategy Papers for achieving the Millennium Development Goals have again raised the importance of information support, for example, to raise awareness of policy makers to the particular needs of the poor in addressing urban poverty (DFID 2001). In addition, an evaluation of DFID's research dissemination reinforced this as a priority issue (WEDC/ITAD 2002).

It is against and out of these concerns that project R7127 has developed. The fact that it was funded is an acknowledgement that KaR research was generally weak in the area of dissemination of project results and outputs. This coincided with a further acknowledgement of the importance of the dissemination of research as a new, important and challenging issue.

Spreading the Word: Phase 1

Project R7127 began in 1998. Its purpose was to research the current understanding of and approaches to the dissemination of research by UK and international agencies engaged in research into water supply and sanitation in low and middle-income countries. Phase 1 was a mainly desk-based study involving a literature review of research dissemination by this and other disciplines; case studies of successful and less successful dissemination activities carried out by a limited number of researchers; and interviews with key DFID research contractors and project managers and others commissioned to carry out research for non-DFID donor agencies.

The main output of Phase 1 was the publication *Spreading the Word: Practical guidelines for research dissemination strategies* (Saywell and Cotton, 1999). This sought to achieve several stated objectives including:

- to further understand current approaches taken by sector-based agencies to the dissemination of research;

- an initial analysis of commonly used dissemination strategies;

- identification of some of the factors that constrain and facilitate the dissemination process; and

- tentative guidelines for those planning a dissemination strategy.

The key findings of the Phase 1 literature review are summarised by Saywell and Cotton (1999, p.3). The main message is that the ongoing dissemination of research is a vital component of any project in the development sector. The most effective approach uses a combination of dissemination formats and pathways, selected for their suitability to address the information needs and resources of the identified target audiences. Assessing the impact of dissemination ensures its continued efficacy, although a distinction is made between the impact of the dissemination method and the affects of the application of the research findings.

Spreading the Word: Phase 2

The limited scope of Phase 1 did not address several critical issues including:

- the need to know about what Southern based information users want (including government, NGOs and other develop-related organisations and personnel such as teachers, students and consultants);

- how to understand the relative merits of different dissemination formats and pathways and the reasons for their successful use; and

- the need for information leading to a better understanding of the potential indicators of the impact of dissemination.

Phase 2 addresses these issues, as described in Section 2.
The main outputs of Phase 2 are:

- *Practice what you preach* (Woodfield 2001), a tracking survey report which documents a clear demand for such research and its associated outputs;

- *Literature review: Dissemination pathways and indicators of impact and development* (Saywell, Woodfield and Cotton, 2001); and

- Consultation processes employed to test and validate the ideas resulting from phase one with a broad audience of Southern information users and providers.

Who should read this book

This book is written with the following readers in mind:

- those commissioned by DFID to carry out research, specifically in the water and sanitation sector, although the guidelines should also have relevance to researchers in other development sectors beyond water and sanitation;

- non-DFID research contractors and other donors who commission research;

- personnel from local government, NGOs and CBOs and private sector firms who are involved in dissemination of research; and

- DFID personnel with formal responsibility or particular interest in research and dissemination issues.

Structure and content of this document

Section 2 comprises a more detailed overview of the methodologies used in phase two of this research, and the elements that are still outstanding. Section 3 presents an analysis of the data organised around five critical themes and associated lessons learned. The final section provides draft guidelines for research contractors with checklists aimed at enabling them to operationalise these guidelines in their own organisation and in relation to their particular research project.

Where to find out more

Further information about the project can be found at the project website at http://www.lboro.ac.uk/departments/cv/wedc/projects/stw/index.htm (Accessed 16/07/03).

The following project reports are available online:

Saywell, D.L. and Cotton, A.P. (1999) *Spreading the Word : Practical Guidelines for Research Dissemination Strategies.* WEDC, Loughborough University. http://www.lboro.ac.uk/departments/cv/wedc/publications/stw.htm (Accessed 16/07/03)

Saywell, D.L., Woodfield, J. and Cotton, A.P. (2000) *Practical Guidelines for Research Dissemination Strategies Phase II – a Literature Review.* WEDC, Loughborough University.

http://www.lboro.ac.uk/departments/cv/wedc/projects/stw/lr6.pdf
(Accessed 16/07/03)

Woodfield, J. (2001) *Practice what you Preach: Phase One Impact Survey Analysis Report*. WEDC, Loughborough University.
http://wedc.lboro.ac.uk/publications/online-catalogue.htm

Section 2

What we have done so far

This project has been a two phase study and this book refers to Phase 2 of the research. The purpose of the second phase was to validate ideas from Phase 1 with a Southern audience of information users and disseminators. A raft of methodological techniques was employed to fulfil the purpose of this second phase. These were predominantly qualitative and are described below.

Phase 1 - Impact survey analysis report: Practice what you preach

This impact survey was carried out approximately two years after the distribution of *Spreading the Word* (1999, Saywell and Cotton). A questionnaire was sent to all recipients identified for the main distribution of this output as recorded in the dissemination log. Its focus covered:

- dissemination pathways used and their appropriateness for the recipient;

- the usefulness and comprehensibility of its content;

- an assessment of the level and nature of use made of this publication; and

- whether and how far the information was shared beyond the original recipient.

The following areas were suggested for further exploration:

- greater reference to the body of available literature; and

- greater focus in terms of content on workshops, seminars and hands-on training, multimedia, dissemination targeting, dealing with disinterested groups, new information communication technologies (ICTs) and the poor, dissemination need and uptake, timescales, and eliciting feedback.

Although *Spreading the Word* was generally well received, there are limitations in both its content and dissemination and consequent lessons to be learned from each of these, which might be usefully applied to subsequent similar activities.

Literature review: Dissemination pathways and indicators of impact and development (2000, Saywell, Woodfield and Cotton)

Building on *Spreading the Word*, this review looked at the different dissemination pathways described in the literature and indictors of dissemination impact, drawing on both development-related and other disciplines. It is worth noting that key points arising included:

- the need for a cyclical model of communication with stakeholders;

- an exploration of the use and usefulness of ICTs versus more traditional methods of knowledge transfer;

- the need to assess users' information use environments (IUEs); and

- the difficulty of identifying reliable indicators of impact.

Southern consultation[1]

To date we have carried out or commissioned overseas partners (in Bangladesh, Colombia and South Africa) to complete the following:

- Key informant interviews with Southern-based users of Northern-based information provision and Southern-based providers of information. A total of 24 interviews were conducted, following a semi-structured interview schedule. 14 of these were commissioned through the in-country collaborating institutions.

- 14 case study surveys of Southern-based users of Northern-based information provision and Southern-based providers of information. These were commissioned by WEDC with the collaborating organisations, following the agreed Terms of Reference.

- In country workshops in Bangladesh, Colombia and South Africa involving Southern-based participants from agencies who are users of Northern-based information provision and who are also providers of information. One workshop was carried out by the WEDC team in each country, in

---

1. For a breakdown of participating organisations by region see Table 1.

collaboration with partners, with five additional workshops organised by the Environment Population Research Centre (EPRC), Bangladesh, following a similar agenda.

Participants of workshops, case studies and key informant interviews are linked to a wide range of organisations: international donor agencies on in-country programmes, government ministries, local government, international and local NGOs, universities, research institutes, religious organisations and community based organisations (CBOs)[2].

Participants' professional roles also cover a wide spectrum from organisation directors, country directors and assistant directors, heads of projects, project managers and co-ordinators, sector specialists and consultants. The professional disciplines represented were predominantly water supply and sanitation service provision, sustainable development, welfare and information management.

Data analysis

The data was gathered as described above, from a range of beneficiaries, most of whom also had an information mediation or dissemination role in their own right. The data was analysed using the *ATLAS ti 4.2* qualitative data analysis programme. From this, it was possible to identify a number of critical themes and lessons learned, and in turn, to develop a set of guidelines.

---

2. For details see Table 1.

Section 3

Critical themes and lessons learned

Introduction

In this section, we present the analysis of the data. The fieldwork covered two aspects of organisational dissemination experience: receiving information and sending it out. The participating organisations all had this dual role. The objectives of their own dissemination and communication programmes varied according to their specific organisational mission but included:

- awareness-raising initiatives and mass education programmes to the community about hygiene education, safe water supply, disaster preparedness and arsenic contamination;

- communication initiatives towards global, national and local level scientific and technical knowledge sharing;

- the development of training modules for partners, stakeholders and users; and

- establishing organisational research needs and priorities.

They were also interested in receiving information that supported their own communication campaigns on these topics.

This section is organised around five critical themes and lessons learned which have emerged from the data analysis. From these, the guidelines in Section 4 are developed.

Dissemination strategies

The institutions taking part in the consultation process varied as to whether or not they had a formal dissemination strategy. A common feature amongst them, however, was that dissemination was seen to be an important element of their work and there were intentions to develop strategies where none already existed. A standard institutional approach to this was generally favoured to provide a generic, comprehensive strategy, but with the flexibility to change and evolve to the needs of particular projects, departments, information content and target audiences.

A recurring theme expressed by those consulted is that the amount of effort spent on designing and conducting research far outweighs the effort put into disseminating the products of it. In Colombia, examples were given of material being published for professional audiences although it was not then known how to go about disseminating it.

Several general principles of an effective dissemination strategy emerged from the consultation process:

1. As part of the need for research, programmes should be demand-driven. The use of appropriate dissemination methods is an important aspect of this and any decisions made about this should be based on what is known about the most appropriate dissemination pathways for direct beneficiaries and research user groups. It is important to distinguish between these two groups, as those for whom the research has a potentially direct impact, and those who use the findings and outputs of research in order to bring about some impact on the lives of beneficiaries.

2. Involvement of different actors who have experience or interest in dissemination enhances the development of a standard approach, through the collective synthesis of approaches to and practice of dissemination. This can include input from different geographic partners as lessons learned in one region may prove to be of value in another. Final decisions about individual cases of dissemination should be taken by those closest to the project and its audiences, such as the project steering committee and wider stakeholders.

3. Internal dissemination should be given equal priority to external dissemination. An area of past neglect, this allows staff members to be cognisant with the innovations, technical development, quality processes etc. of the organisation, and in turn to be able to promote the organisation effectively to those outside of it.

4. The main characteristics of a dissemination strategy should relate to the project objectives, the selected target audiences to be influenced and their characteristics (e.g. education level, information demands and resources, consumption patterns), affordability and financial viability for the chosen duration, and added value associated with it (potential for re-use and its application to wider audiences).

Box 3.1. Key lessons on dissemination strategies

A generic, organisational dissemination strategy, which can be amended to suit different purposes is the most effective mechanism

Dissemination planning is best informed by carrying out a user needs' assessment of the target audiences whom researchers seek to influence

Using the experience of all individuals involved in dissemination within an organisation leads to a comprehensive strategy

Internal dissemination is a necessary element of a dissemination strategy as it strengthens overall capacity in this area

---

Target audience

Saywell and Cotton (1999) provide some guidance on the appropriate dissemination pathways for different audiences[3]. Phase Two of Spreading the Word tested these assumptions using the in-country consultation methods already described and provided empirical evidence in support of them as well as bringing alternative and new concepts to light. The target audiences featured in these discussions were wide ranging from municipality staff to local farmers[4] (see Table 2).

The key to developing an understanding of the target audience is to know as much as possible about the impact of cultural aspects, which may operate at either a social or an organisational level, or both. However, as well as these mainly behavioural factors, there are other resource-centred considerations.

Socio-cultural factors

It was generally seen to be important to find out as much as possible about the target audience. A formal needs assessment would focus on the 'information use environments' (IUEs) (Menou, 2000) of users i.e. what do they know and what do they want to know?; how do they communicate best?; how does information flow through the group?; how do they receive information? Sometimes it is useful in this respect to explore the use of mainstream and traditional dissemination channels as these are based on common cultural practice. For example, in Bangladesh, the PROKASH project targets women as the main proponent of change in family status and behaviour. It is claimed that women

---

3. Saywell, D.L. and Cotton, A.P. (1999) Table 4, pp. 54-55
4. Schilderman's study (2002) looks at meeting demand for knowledge and information by the urban poor and provides further useful guidance.

prefer to attend a 'family session' in which women and children are informed about a particular issue such as the health and social benefits of drinking tubewell water and installing sanitary latrines. It is stated that it is usually inappropriate to use printed materials for these women as only teachers, students and some NGO staff members have the level of education required for this.

This necessitates an effort on behalf of the project team to familiarise itself with basic facts which may be difficult to ascertain from a position outside of the target audience community. Still it is important to verify that traditional channels are, in fact, the best means of disseminating the information held, and to check that assumptions about them are still based on the current situation. In South Africa, for example, it was learned from Mvula Trust that a growing trend in the popularity of cartoons and illustrations makes them a more effective tool than written materials which require time and effort to read.

Other issues to be aware of are the content and language of the materials, which again should be informed by what is known about the target audience. For instance, using particular terminology may alienate certain groups as cited in South Africa, where race and racial linguistic practice was raised as a potential source of alienation. A simple way in which dissemination can be integrated in the main communication channels is by using accessible language.

Another aspect of cultural concern is how the information we want to convey relates to local problems and demands. If the project is demand-responsive and target audience participation has been a factor at each stage of conducting the research, this is relatively guaranteed. However, research findings can have relevance to a wider audience (of different professional levels, regions etc) than was foreseen at the project proposal stage. This will involve creating and disseminating different versions of research outputs for the different audiences, again based on known socio-cultural factors.

This all assumes that identified users will want to know about and be receptive to our research findings. It is not enough that we deem it to be 'for their own good' and believe it will lead to beneficial outcomes for them. So what about uninterested users? This point was raised at the Johannesburg workshop. There are basic measures that can be taken to encourage a positive reaction to information, such as ensuring local relevance of content and checking the best format is used to send it in. However it may be the case that users are prejudiced against a particular issue or do not recognise the value of the information to them and in this case, the message or the channel used is irrelevant due to their preconceptions. This can be improved by disseminating information through a trustworthy source or 'infomediary' (see p.18). Users' fear of change must also be recognised. Demonstration projects can be useful in allaying such anxieties. The words of a Colombian community water supply and sanitation works committee member offer insight into this:

"The most important thing is sensitisation of the people, so people can learn to love what they have. This is the first thing. If people don't love what they have, it is impossible to give them knowledge".

Resource issues

The South African workshop raised the point that the dissemination preferences of the communicator can influence the choice of the channel or methodology used, in spite of the actual resources available to users. For instance, writers of a facilitation workbook might assume that users have access to scissors, glue or paper. Similarly, dissemination based on new ICTs may be unsuitable for those without the infrastructural resources to support this. A further factor that was identified in the consultation were the needs of people with disabilities who may require specific formats delivered via dissemination pathways that do not disadvantage this group.

Box 3.2. Key lessons on target audiences

A formal target audience information needs assessment (including an understanding of relevant socio-cultural factors) provides information on what information (content, style, resource requirements and language) should be provided and the way in which it should be delivered

Ensuring local relevance of information results in increased receptiveness by audiences

Different local versions of information can be produced based on user needs analysis data

---

Pathways

We have already outlined the socio-cultural and resource-based principles that determine choice of dissemination pathway. Table 2 collates the information gathered in consultation with Southern users and information providers, on proven and suggested successful dissemination methods set against target audiences. These pathways reflect experience and good practice, i.e. what respondents currently use or have used in the past and found to be effective.

Several of those interviewed also carried out either user information needs' analysis or some form of monitoring and evaluation of dissemination methods used.

Some general observations can be made from the data contained in Table 2. At policy and decision making level, the main suggested routes for dissemination are written materials, from fax to posters and books. The range of methods used for this group is probably the broadest of all the groups and includes electronic, official documentation, training, flyers and T-shirts. Predictably, journal publication is key to dissemination to the scientific research community, with additional benefits being found in other participatory educational and training methods such as workshops, conferences and seminars. It should be noted, however, that many academics in low and middle-income countries do not enjoy easy access to peer reviewed journals. Those involved in the research itself need regular updates of progress, which are likely to be internal documentation from the project as well as the wider dissemination pathways cited. Dissemination to practitioner level covers a range of training and participatory pathways, as well as written materials such as sector journals and newsletters. The range of pathways aimed at communities and potential project beneficiaries is the most extensive and covers many kinds of educational techniques (school, educational community sessions), entertainment-based methods (folk theatre and puppetry), use of the media (radio, TV) and face-to-face interaction (tea stall sessions, community project worker-led activities). The community which is actually impacted upon by the project will have greater and more personalised feedback of progress and involvement with the project.

In general terms, a mix of media (electronic, hard copy and face-to-face) was found to provide the best strategy to reach the broadest possible audience. An example of this was given by UNICEF Bangladesh Urban Slums Programme of the 'multiple channel dissemination approach' in which a raft of dissemination options are available, matched for their appropriateness based on the needs of the target audience. A rigorous methodological approach was incorporated into this model through the stages of strategy design, materials development, pretesting, piloting and finalising materials based on continuous feedback and evaluation.

The following section provides examples and discussion of the use of some of these methods.

The mass media

The consultation process provided examples of the way in which the success of different dissemination pathways depends on the information culture that pervades in any given location. For example, in Colombia, state-run and controlled television was perceived to be an unreliable dissemination medium. An exception to this is a reported information campaign against a cholera epidemic in which television and radio proved especially useful in reaching the mass public. However, an evaluation of this campaign showed that individual visits by 'medical' personnel were more effective. The reasons given for this were that it was likely to be the only visit that families ever had from such an authority figure and that there was a strong oral tradition in the culture. In Peru, however, the reverse is true and local television broadcasts were reported to be a very common form of awareness-raising about local issues. Certain cultural norms apply here too as TV programmes in Peru should be no longer than 20 minutes, with the camera focusing on the subject of the report rather than the presenter. In Celendin, Peru, an effective community-projects marketing exercise is a regular event on the day before a major festival.

However, the media as a vehicle for dissemination of research should be used with caution. There was evidence of a lack of scientific correspondents capable of covering stories involving the simplification of technical details for a general audience. Consequently, such features are either not run or provide incorrect information.

The Internet

Loading information onto the Internet has the potential to reach a huge international audience, but the consultation process reinforced the fact that its value to Southern information users is far less than we might assume (supported by Schilderman 2002). Web access was noted to be problematic in all the regions consulted, being most severe at community level. An additional difficulty is that web-based information rarely appears in accessible local languages such as Bangla. Online policy papers were said to seldom reach municipalities due to a lack of computing facilities, the means to download information and technical skills. Despite this, there is a strong perception that electronic information is the way forward and plans were outlined to supply all Bangladeshi government officials with access to a PC, as these are presently available at district but not at local level. A further example of this is the development of online services based in resource centres and cyber cafes providing access by children to global information produced by national networks which was also underway in Bangladesh supported by the UNDP Sustainable Development Network Programme.

Traditional communication channels

The potential use of mainstream channels of communication with audiences having a strong oral tradition has been raised already. There are many examples of this in Table 2. Consultation revealed that face-to-face communication may often be the most effective method of informing people, although the process can be expensive and can only reach a limited group of people. As Table 2 shows, this is mostly used at community level where it can include public theatre, post-religious gatherings for women and adolescents, men's tea stall sessions and children's games.

Institutional dissemination

A very diverse range of dissemination pathways was purportedly used to communicate at an institutional level, from T shirts and caps to newsletters and conferences. Obviously this will depend on the disseminating organisation, the message, and the sort of professional institution to be reached. Clearly though, there are many more ways of getting research findings across to donor, policy-making, intermediary and practitioner organisations than simply writing reports. Methods that are commonly used in the North for research dissemination may have limited international relevance. For example, journal subscriptions and the costs of attending conferences, especially international events were said to be prohibitive to Southern information users, although the information was valued.

Mvula Trust gave some examples of effective organisational dissemination such as the *Mvula Local Government Water and Sanitation Diary*. This has a distribution list of 8000 and is well received and used by local government councillors and officials, MVULA staff, NGOs, partners, consultants and fieldworkers. The bi-monthly *South African Water Bulletin* is a further example of a free dissemination output. It is produced in both hard and electronic copies plus a CD ROM version. This has a more popular focus than the *Water South Africa*, Water Resource Commission's subscription-based scientific journal of original research.

Using infomediaries

The use of an infomediary to act as mediator between the originator of the information and potential users can be very useful, and can mitigate against some of the problems associated with uninterested and unknown users, as already described.

Related to this, these are some of the points that emerged from the consultation process. Infomediaries should be carefully selected according to the following criteria. They should:

- have a clear definition and understanding of the intended audience;
- have high potential coverage of intended audiences, e.g. be part of an intermediary network for extended dissemination;
- be well known and trusted by the intended audience;
- be convinced of the message they are sharing;
- provide language adaptations for local audiences;
- provide content adaptations for non-specialist audiences;
- have access to sufficient resources to carry out an effective campaign; and
- receive regular training.

The Urban Slum Project in Comilla, Bangladesh (DPHE and UNICEF) is an example of successful infomediary collaboration. Ten field motivators cover the target audience of 200 slum dwelling families and attend a ninety minute training session twice a month.

On a larger scale, the Sanitation and Family Education Resource (SAFER) Project (DPHE and UNICEF) in Dhaka, disseminates its experience through planned workshops with 160 non-partner NGOs over the five years project duration.

Viability and funding issues

Many barriers to successful dissemination have been discussed so far, such as the lack of knowledge about how to achieve this and about target audience needs, socio-cultural and resource-based considerations, user access to ICTs, uninterested users, racial barriers, language and regional barriers and so on. However, the most significant barrier reported is the lack of sufficient funding to implement the proposed activities and to ensure their continuance for their intended duration. Researchers based in the North may also experience cases when dissemination costs are not seen to be a priority. What is clear is that dissemination at any level has a price attached to it and in order to meet objectives, adequate funds need to be provided.

Amongst the general difficulties, publishing and printing costs, paying intermediaries to disseminate information, and the costs associated with

---

Box 3.3. Key lessons on dissemination pathways

A multiple channel dissemination approach reaches the broadest audience

The mass media can be a useful mass dissemination pathway, if a corresponding information culture prevails in which research and information is distributed in this way

The potential of electronic information is recognised but this should be supplemented by other dissemination approaches

Dissemination methods found to be used successfully in the South but used less frequently by Northern researchers can provide valuable opportunities to reach target audiences.

A useful route of assess to target audiences is through infomediaries although careful selection is important

---

participatory and workshop methods were most commonly cited. In Latin America, it is not usual for information to be paid for by users, thereby requiring alternative sources of funding to be found. The problem is double-edged, however, as it was noted that information which is provided free of charge, such as the WRC's *Water South Africa* journal, is not always perceived to have equal credibility as 'paid for' information.

One attempted solution to this problem was the formation of the Streams of Knowledge Global Coalition partnership. As one member says

"There are some commonalities between the centres that form the partnership. You have probably observed that, for example, when you try to do something, really getting the right partnership arrangement, makes it more interesting and more sustainable in a sense. Because there is a constant feed, without having to pay for it. You get access to information which we don't have to really source ourselves" (Emcali, Colombia).

The importance of effective networking emerged as key to viable dissemination for the proposed duration and as a partial solution to a lack of adequate funding.

Another example of best practice in this area is the CALDAS Network, launched by the Colombian Institute for Science and Technology Development (COLCIENCIAS) Colombia. It is aimed at scientists, researchers, students and innovators, with the purpose of linking them into the scientific and technological activities of the country through thematic networks, electronic mailing lists and virtual talk forums.

Box 3.4. Key lessons on viability and funding issues

Insufficient funding is the main barrier to a viable dissemination strategy and accurate costs assessment is a means of avoiding these difficulties

There may be cultural associations attached to the issue of paying for information

Use of networks provides a means of strengthening the viability of a dissemination strategy for the chosen period

---

Impact issues

Measuring the impact of dissemination is recognised as being problematic (Saywell and Cotton 1999, Schilderman 2002). Nevertheless, there were several examples in which monitoring and evaluation of dissemination was occurring in the participating organisations, although there were differing definitions of this. This section is based on this experience.

Methods

Examples of both qualitative and quantitative methods used include:

- questionnaires sent with publications (e.g. the Mvula Trust diary questionnaire focused on factors such as usefulness, design, layout and relevance);

- using PHAST and other participatory methods and tools e.g. taking materials to communities for feedback as part of an iterative design process;

- monitoring the ways in which other agencies use the materials and any amendments made to them;

- constant user needs assessment; and

- focused discussion.

Pre-testing of intended dissemination methods is recommended prior to their use. Piloting procedures can confirm whether our assumptions about the information needs and resources of our target audiences are correct.

Indicators of dissemination success

The difficulties of measuring dissemination impact was noted by many of the organisations, as it necessitates the need to 'get inside' the target audience, be they an organisation or an individual.

When talking about indicators of dissemination success, there was some inevitable confusion between and overlap with indicators of the successful *uptake of the message* disseminated. Some firmly believed this to be a sensible proxy measure of dissemination success as effective communication must precede uptake. Examples of this are:

- assessment of the knowledge level on a topic (e.g. measured through training events; Colombian works committee monitored knowledge level of community members of the functioning of their water supply system);

- promotion of women to higher positions within an organisation;

- behaviour change used such as evidence of using sanitary facilities and practising hand washing;

- looking for cases in which policy development has been influenced by the content of materials disseminated;

- evidence of problem-solving based on outputs;

- quality of contributors to journals; and

- quality of students on training courses.

Generally, in these cases, measuring the value of the information to the recipient and any beneficial effects was used as an indicator that dissemination has worked.

Other successful attempts were being made to measure more directly the effectiveness, appropriateness and reach of particular dissemination methods, but these were far less frequent. These indicators include:

- levels of demand for the information from other sources;

- frequency and nature of information use; and

- awareness of any dissemination outputs from any particular knowledge provider.

In addition, it is useful to measure the information flow through target audiences. An example of a two year stockpile of books at CINARA was given as an indication that that flow was not being achieved, the reason being in this case, that it was felt that there were insufficient skills relating to dissemination in the organisation. Information is in danger of becoming out of date over time, reinforcing the case for timely and effective dissemination of research findings.

Box 3.5. Key lessons on impact issues

The various dissemination monitoring and evaluation techniques should be pre-tested prior to use

Indicators of successful uptake of the message are often perceived to be indicators of successful dissemination practice. A combination of direct and proxy indicators such as these can provide an acceptable measure of how well we have reached our target audience

---

Concluding remarks

This section has described the five critical themes resulting from the data analysis and the associated lessons learned. In addition, there are some wider points which have emerged strongly from the consultation process, which provide pointers to ways in which dissemination could be further strengthened.

1. There is an expressed need for a peer group network of those involved in disseminating research, to share experience and learning in this area. It was noted after each consultation workshop that there was a strong general desire to keep the lines of communication open with WEDC and with the other workshop attendees, to receive further documentation and outputs relating to this and to develop new initiatives. This suggests that Southern stakeholders feel isolated in this particular area of their work.

2. The need was expressed for a tool that formalises what is known about best practice of each dissemination method, such as workshops, conferences, and the many different types of publications. This mirrors the findings of the *Evaluation of DFID's Research Dissemination* (WEDC/ITAD 2002) that

researchers may be specialists in their field but are far less likely to be experts in knowledge management and dissemination techniques.

The need for appropriate incentives for researchers to disseminate their research effectively was raised. In the case of Latin America it was stated that the importance of dissemination is not widely recognised and there are few incentives to carry this out. In terms of KaR research, DFID has an important role to play in providing a supportive framework. Addressing points one and two above, could go part way to providing a solution to this lack of incentives.

Section 4

Preliminary guidelines for research contractors

In this section we present a set of preliminary guidelines on dissemination for research contractors based on the critical themes and key lessons outlined in the previous section. Although these are intended for those planning a dissemination strategy for a new project, they also have relevance for those who have reached a mid-way stage in their research, or are at the end of their project and are seeking to extend the reach of any dissemination intended. They are meant to be guidelines rather than a prescriptive formula, as it is recognised that the context of each research project can vary widely, necessitating different strategic approaches to the dissemination of findings. Experience of what works also plays a part in successful dissemination and lessons will certainly be learned on the way.

Guideline 1: Adopt a strategic approach to dissemination

General thinking is towards an acceptance of the need for a strategic approach to dissemination rather than treating it on an ad hoc basis. Organisational dissemination strategies offer more than lots of individual strategies for each project as there are potential benefits of sharing our experience of reaching target audiences and of aggregating outputs for dissemination wherever possible. Where it is feasible for an organisation to achieve this, by bringing together different researchers and those interested in dissemination, a framework based on what been has found to work can be designed. It should be noted that internal dissemination is a vital part of an effective overall strategy.

A more standardised institutional approach, where relevant, needs to be flexible enough to allow for adaptation to the circumstances, outputs and target audience needs and resources related to each project. These decisions about individual projects should be taken by the project team, steering committee and its various stakeholders. It is they who are likely to possess the most accurate local knowledge about these factors.

Box 4.1. Checklist 1

Organisational level

1. Review existing organisational dissemination practice:

- Carry out an information audit, focusing on the way in which staff understand dissemination, what current practice is and what has been found to work successfully, matching dissemination pathways to target audience. Collate the results of this to form a framework for dissemination for use by others

- Identify which audience groups the organisation needs to influence and where it needs to target advocacy materials

- Relate dissemination to the organisational mission, as this increases its perceived value and the priority given to it.

Project level

1. The planning team should include project team and steering committee members, and wider stakeholders and interested parties as appropriate

2. Plan and integrate a dissemination strategy into the project life cycle, by identifying when optimum opportunities are presented for dissemination during the project cycle

3. Identify priority areas of need i.e. who will the intended users be (i.e. those who use research to benefit the poor) and who will the beneficiaries of research outputs be (i.e. those for whom the research has a potentially direct impact). It is important to distinguish between these two groups and the extent to which you are able to assess demand from one or both of these. The data collected in this study was both from those working directly with end user beneficiaries and those working with users of research who in turn were working with beneficiaries

4. Decide who will be responsible for co-ordinating dissemination activities. Plan to use a graduated model of proposed research outputs, which each have increasing detail, complexity and technical specialisation, as appropriate for the target audience

5. Provide detailed costings for each element of the dissemination activities, as a dedicated amount for dissemination.

Guideline 2: Know your target audience

A dissemination strategy requires certain elements to be known relating to target groups. An important factor in determining who are the target audiences of research, is the subject matter of the research itself. The subject will determine the geographic regions and locations of target audiences where research findings are relevant, both where the research was carried out and beyond. Factors such as the extent to which the research focuses on practical applications in the field, organisational issues or has state level policy implications has a bearing on the selection of target groups and the type of output which should be disseminated to them.

Once target groups are chosen, it is important to find out about audience information use environments (IUEs) which may be costly in terms of time, but disseminating information is also an expensive process. To miss the target because the aim is inaccurate or to use the wrong tool to reach it, results in wasted effort and expense.

Awareness of socio-cultural factors is key to an understanding of target audience IUEs. Unless these are known, it is impossible to be sure of the appropriate content, format and pathway in which to send information. These factors will also vary significantly across regions and what is common practice in one location may not be useful elsewhere. It is useful to examine the use of traditional and mainstream information and communication channels for our own dissemination purposes, whilst not assuming that these will be the most effective vehicle.

Another important aspect of assessing users' IUEs is to know about the level and types of resources at their disposal. These factors have an important bearing on decisions made about formats in which information is presented and dissemination pathways used.

Uninterested users should not be forgotten although they may be hard to reach. Information needs to be locally relevant, possibly using an infomediary who is known to them to demonstrate the potential impact of the message.

Box 4.2. Checklist 2

1. The target audience is made up of the groups of key organisations that you want to influence and that you want to act on your research. It might also include direct beneficiaries of your research, if the scope of your dissemination strategy and the capacity of the research team extends this far. Draft a list of your proposed target audiences, working in collaboration with in-country partners if possible, to review and verify the list. This list is dependent on the research topic and which groups are to be influenced by the findings.

2. Carry out a user information needs analysis (e.g. by questionnaire or interview survey), taking into consideration the points listed below:

- What it is that the poor or agencies representing/assisting them need to know?

- How is that need demonstrated? Are there any indicators?

- Is the research strictly relevant to the local context and is it perceived by potential users to be relevant?

- How do users of the research need to use the information (manual, guidance notes, algorithm)?

- What resources (skills, knowledge, and money) do users need to make use of that information?

- What is the most appropriate information format e.g. the length of document, written style, language, non-written format for each target group?

- What level of detailed content is appropriate (dependent on the depth of understanding of the issues required by those the project seeks to influence)?

- What is the preferred means of dissemination, based on an understanding of locally available options?

- This can be supplemented by data contained in the organisational dissemination strategy (see Checklist One).

3. Work with in-country partners to identify potential uninterested users. Consider how to ensure that research outputs have a local relevance to their situation and engage appropriate intermediary organisations, who have close knowledge of these groups, to construct a strategy aimed at awareness raising in these groups.

Guideline 3: Hitting the target

A multi-channel approach to dissemination is most likely to hit the identified audience. This approach is also effective in reaching a broad range of audiences and beneficiaries, since a single version of content, presented in a single format and sent via a single pathway is unlikely to have general relevance on any of these counts.

In order to reach a wide general audience, consider using the mass media. However, before tapping into this as a potential dissemination vehicle, check how it is used in a particular location and ascertain what it is and is not effective for.

Use of ICTs in their various forms depends on the level of associated local resources. While we should be cautious in our assumptions about these, we also need to be aware that ICTs have an actual and growing potential in sometimes unlikely locations. Before discounting their use, we need to ascertain what the local situation is.

According to fieldwork evidence, as UK researchers, we need to stand back from our own usual methods of disseminating research to organisations and to consider less conventional methods used by in-country agencies. Table 2 shows a range of methods used to get messages across to local government and NGOs for example. We need to be creative and adventurous in our choice of dissemination pathways, within the limitations which deadlines and budgets impose, and provided we have assessed the appropriateness of our method.

The important role played by infomediaries cannot be underestimated. The local knowledge they possess of IUEs and local needs, of organisations and communities, plus their perceived standing with target groups is invaluable. They can provide the entry point that may evade the researcher. Involving stakeholders from the outset of the project who can act as infomediaries whenever a message needs to be relayed is one way of ensuring success.

Box 4.3. Checklist 3

1. Review what is known about the target audiences in terms of their information needs (to help guide the content), and the best ways in which to send them information (to help with decisions about which dissemination pathways to use).

2. Decide what is the function of the dissemination output at a particular point in the project cycle and what function it is to serve, e.g. is it to act as publicity, to generate feedback, or to communicate findings? This will aid decisions about the content (i.e. how detailed or technical does it need to be? what length should it be?).

3. Make imaginative use of all available and relevant pathways including conventional methods (journal article publications), opportunities for interpersonal communication (conference and workshop forums), using information and communication technologies (e-conferencing and the World Wide Web) and more traditional methods which allow the poor more easy access to information (posters and radio broadcasts). For more detailed suggestions, based on the data gathered, see Table 2.

4. A far-reaching dissemination strategy in which communications flow extends horizontally to the academic community and funding bodies, 'downwards' to NGOs, practitioners and the poor, while at the same time providing channels for 'upwards' communication and participation, is likely to mean that the classic research report has very limited use, as it is generally lengthy and unfocused. Conversely, face-to-face communication brings research to life in a very unique way. Whatever media are chosen, the link between pathway and audience needs to be clear.

5. Researchers need to be aware of these to ensure that certain audiences are not disadvantaged by any outputs produced and that equal weight is given to each dissemination output.

6. Depending on the nature of the dissemination exercise, the range of outputs should be as broad as possible for the maximum reach. The basic message should be adapted to the needs of the different audiences, with varying levels of detail and technical information. Some questions to ask of our chosen format are:

Checklist 3 *(continued)*

- Is it accessible to intended users?
- Are there alternative and/or additional media which would better facilitate accessibility and comprehension?
- Is it cost-effective?
- Is personal interaction a possibility?
- Is the medium simple?
- Are electronic media supplemented by paper-based versions?

7. Consideration should be given to the use of possible infomediaries in providing communication channels. Things to consider are:

- Is the source perceived to be competent, experienced and having credible motives?
- What is its relationship to other trusted sources?
- Is it sensitive to the concerns of the users?
- Is it oriented towards dissemination and knowledge use?
- Has appropriate use been made of infomediaries with established relationships with intended audiences?

8. Consider the following general content issues:

- Include a summary – a separate summary of main findings and recommendations
- Make information accessible. Shape your material so that it is accessible to different stakeholders, showing how it relates to their concerns, while remaining true to the perceptions and priorities of our research population
- Be clear. Emphasise key findings for action
- State which problems are common and which are serious
- Provide solid evidence to support your views
- Avoid too much detail
- Identify key policy messages
- Make recommendations practical.

Guideline 4: A viable strategy

Research dissemination is not a one-off event. Ideally it should involve initial announcements and awareness raising, interim and 'final' outputs plus possible further updates and evaluations of impact and uptake of the findings. In order for a programme of dissemination to continue for the chosen duration, all associated costs should be itemised in the research proposal and agreed for these purposes.

Taking advantage of existing networking initiatives can achieve a high and cost effective level of information sharing with certain interested groups. Time should be spent identifying both regional and international networks relevant to the research as part of the dissemination strategy.

Ideally, any dissemination strategy should include plans for monitoring and evaluation (M & E) of these activities (see Guideline Five below). From the researcher's point of view, this is an important way of checking the effectiveness of existing practice and adapting future dissemination tasks accordingly. An additional benefit is the potential for continuance of projects where appropriate if funders are made aware of the returns on their investment.

Box 4.4. Checklist 4

1. The following are some of the actions that can be used to contribute towards a viable dissemination strategy:
- continuing to publish in the area after the end of the project
- supporting change activities in the community, based upon the concluded research
- monitoring government and NGOs' progress on action points arising out of the project
- taking part in relevant national/international meetings
- holding meetings with key relevant stakeholders to review progress.

2. End-users can themselves achieve lasting improvements by influencing policy development. This can be done in several ways including:
- taking part in national meetings
- supporting work by other groups around issues that are of concern to the end-user group. For example, the beneficiaries of a new sanitation intervention promoting this intervention to a second group who are beneficiaries in a health project.

3. Identify appropriate national, regional, local and thematic networks, which can act as conduits for project output dissemination.

Guideline 5: What have we achieved?

Despite the problems inherent in attempting to monitor and evaluate the impact of our dissemination activities, it is important that we do so, in order to build our own body of knowledge about our information users and how to reach them successfully. We can then share this information within our own organisation, or with other interested networks. A range of methods has been suggested by participating organisations that have been shown to yield results.

What is also clear is that given the methodological difficulties of distinguishing between the message uptake and the use of appropriate dissemination pathway, we should first pilot our chosen method to confirm that we know what it is we are measuring.

Proxy measures of dissemination effectiveness are often used and provide useful data that arguably reflects dissemination success. Analysis of impact and uptake of research is key to any project and it seems sensible therefore that efforts towards quantifying these factors can also be used to tell us something about whether we are getting dissemination right. If we combine this with more direct measures of dissemination effectiveness in ways suggested by our participants, we will have a combined rich source of data.

Box 4.5. Checklist 5

1. Data can be collected on the effectiveness of a dissemination strategy by asking the following questions:
- Were the messages/materials produced?
- Were they disseminated?
- Did the target audience receive the messages?
- If received, does the target audience remember the message?
- If remembered, how were these messages used?

Other considerations might be:
- The strengths and weaknesses of the dissemination process (this should include negative results)
- Outcomes which can be attributed to the dissemination process
- Recommendations for change and modification to the dissemination process
- The impact on target audiences
- Variations in impact on audiences according to variables of the group, content, context, medium and information source
- Recommendations for further action regarding the evaluation of impact of dissemination.

2. It is important that the timing of any monitoring and evaluation (M&E) or tracking activities is correct. It is difficult to issue general guidelines, which can be widely applied. The researchers on a particular project are likely to be best placed to judge when this should occur, given their knowledge of the target audiences and the nature of the message delivered. A balance needs to be struck between evaluating before the full impact can be assessed, but not so late that those affected are no longer involved or able to be contacted.

3. Ensure that M & E activities are listed in the dissemination strategy at the beginning of any project (see Table 4). At this stage, dissemination objectives should be clearly defined, (although additional effects may become apparent as the project progresses) and the different M & E processes should be timetabled. A range of both qualitative and quantitative indicators may be necessary to verify the demand for and supply of outputs and to identify the use made of disseminated materials.

Checklist 5 (*continued*)

4. The ways in which the results of the M & E will be used should also be agreed in the planning stages. The final documentation should be distributed to the group or should contribute to an organisational knowledge bank of M & E. Suggested ways in which these might then be used (outlined by Gosling and Edwards 1998) are:

   • To provide a discussion framework for the further development of work
   • To inform decisions about dissemination
   • To be the basis for broader dissemination strategies
   • To be a model for subsequent review and evaluation activities
   • To influence other collaborating organisations.

Concluding remarks

These guidelines and checklists are based on the data produced in consultation workshops, interviews and case studies with Southern agencies, and are consolidated by the project literature review and impact analysis survey. They are based on conditions which occur in the different locations and on what has been proven through experience to have some element of success, from which we can learn and improve our own dissemination practice.

The points included in the five checklists are intended to provide some direction for researchers on the implementation of the guidelines and suggestions of how to proceed and what to consider along the way. It is intended that dissemination should be viewed as an organisational issue, and that the actions listed should be applied at an institutional and strategic level. For those who are not supported by an institution or whose organisation does not operate at this level, it is hoped that individual research projects and researchers can usefully implement some or all of these guidelines, to strengthen the dissemination activities associated with their work, and to enjoy the added benefits which accrue from this.

Tables

Table 1. Participating organisations

Name of organisation	Location	Organisation type
EMCALI	Cali, Colombia	Utility
Community Works Committee	Cali, Colombia	CBO
Colombian Institute for Science & Technology/ Development – Colciencias	Cali, Colombia	Research institute
Drinking Water & Basic Sanitation Ministry	Cali, Colombia	Government Ministry
Instituto de Investigación y Desarrollo en Agua Potable, Saneamiento Básico y Conservación del Recurso Hidrico (CINARA)	Cali, Colombia	Research institute/NGO
Programme of Integral and Organised Transfer of Technology on Water Supply Systems (TRANSCOL)	Colombia	Research Institute
University of Antioquia, Colombia	Colombia	Educational institute
Centre of Multidisciplinary Research for Development (CIMDER) Colombia	Colombia	Research Institute
Technological University of Pereira (UTP) Colombia	Colombia	Educational institute
Mayor of municipality of Celendin, Peru	Celendin, Peru	Municipality
National Service of Training (SENA) Colombia	Colombia	Educational institute
Institute CINARA (Research & Development Institute on Water Supply, Sanitation and Water Resources Conservation) Colombia	Colombia	Educational institute
Institute of Statistical Research and Training (ISRT), University of Dhaka.	Dhaka, Bangladesh	University
International Development Enterprises	Dhaka, Bangladesh	Consultant
DFID	Bangladesh	International agency
Sanitation and Family Education Resource Project (SAFER)	Chittagong / Dhaka, Bangladesh	NGO
Disaster Management Bureau	Dhaka, Bangladesh	NGO
UNICEF	Dhaka, Bangladesh	International NGO

Table 1. Participating organisations *(continued)*

UNDP	Bangladesh	International agency
CARITAS	Bangladesh	NGO
SDC (Swiss)	Bangladesh	International NGO
Name unknown	Srinagar, Bangladesh	Religious organisation
IDE Bangladesh	Bangladesh	Research institute
Urban Slum Project by DPHE and UNICEF	Comilla, Bangladesh	International NGO
PROKASS	Bangladesh	NGO
Upazilla Health and Family Welfare Centre	Comilla, Bangladesh	NGO
Institute for Democracy in South Africa (IDASA)	South Africa	NGO
MVULA Trust	South Africa	NGO
Rand Water	South Africa	Utility provider
South African Local Government Association (SALGA)	South Africa	Local government
Water Research Commission (WRC)	South Africa	Research Institute
Department for Water and Forestry Affairs (DWAF), South Africa	South Africa	Water Ministry
Water Support Service Unit (WSSU), South Africa	South Africa	NGO
National Sanitation Co-ordination Committee (NASCO) South Africa	South Africa	NGO
Institute for democracy in South Africa (IDASA)	South Africa	NGO
Witwatersrand University, South Africa	South Africa	Educational institution
Private consultant	South Africa	Consultant

Table 2. Dissemination pathways used[1]

Target audience	Dissemination pathway	Reasons to disseminate findings	What findings are needed and why
Decision-making level Government staff /Policy makers Local government staff and councillors Municipality personnel Water utilities Donor agencies	Fax, letters, telegrams Banners Manuals/books Pamphlets/flyers, Posters Organisation newsletter, Journals, Magazines CD ROM Bibliographic database Internet, Email Videos, DVD Summary project report Workshops/ training sessions Training programme manuals Council meetings and forums Conferences Enquiry service Consultancy T-shirts and caps	• Receive information • Disseminate lessons • Support future policy and action	• Full results and summary for analysis of lessons learned and policy making
Research and project level University staff Research community Project stakeholders/partners	Project reports Publications Professional organisation newsletters Specialist magazines, Local and international journals Networks Internet, Email Dialogue Training programmes Workshops, Seminars, Conferences	*To those directly involved with the research:* • Responsibility for project implementation and monitoring community decision making and action *For the wider scientific community:* • Receive information and build on research in the design of further studies • Adding to the knowledge base	• Regular flow of findings to be able to monitor project, make decisions and adjustments, plan • Full scientific results

Table 2. Dissemination pathways used[1] *(continued)*

Practitioner level Practitioners Sector organisations NGO staff Consultants	Newsletter Posters Journals Magazines Letters Internet, Emails Telephone, Fax Media Bibliographic database Enquiry service Face to face conversation Networks Subject interest group subscription Training modules Workshops Drama T-shirts and caps	• Receive information • Disseminate lessons • Support future policy, action and involvement	• Full results and summary for analysis of lessons learned, advocacy and policy making
Community level Community members Community Based Organisations Students & Adolescents Local farmers Traditional leaders & Imams	Participatory action learning methods Education sessions led by field motivators. School lessons/curricula Demonstrations School information centre Targeted training sessions Imams- using set of posters Local artists Folk songs, Folk theatre, Puppetry Road shows Games Tea stalls Courtyard sessions Family sessions (three or so individuals) Door-to-door visits Battery operated dolls Posters, Articles in newspapers, Magazines Volunteer intermediaries Project workers in community Community committee NGO workers Focus group discussions Radio TV and cable TV Cyber cafes Mobile phones	*For wider community not necessarily involved in the project:* Access to local information and research which has the potential to affect the community *For community members directly involved in the research project:* • To facilitate full participation in the planning, implementation, monitoring and dissemination of project	• Summary of results to create interest and support for projects Awareness-raising materials Community education materials Fuller periodic summary of results so that they can continue to have a key involvement

1. This table includes information from Saywell and Cotton (1999), Table 4

Table 3. Dissemination pathways: comparison of relative advantages and disadvantages[1]

Pathway	Notes	Advantage/s	Disadvantage/s
Working documents	• Concept notes, field diaries, and reports for internal use and the wider research community	• May target research findings to particular groups	• Problems with limited access
Research reports	• Detailed summary of research to satisfy funding requirements or those with high level understanding of subject	• Provides a single reference point for all aspects of the research	• Assumes report read by single audience group • May be written in inaccessible manner
Academic, refereed journal	• Directed at research community.	• Informs scientific community of findings; citations lead to wider impact on intellectual networks	• Limited audience • May be written in an inaccessible manner • Lacks practical orientation
Professional journal	• Directed at practitioner community.	• Reaches a wide practitioner oriented community	• Academic rigour may be lower than refereed journal
Stand alone text book	• Educational model - influencing practice through higher education courses	• Potential to impact on wide audience • Potential to influence development professionals	• Difficulty in accessing key texts in Southern countries • Not practice oriented
Conference, workshop, seminar	• Face to face contact with peers on specific subject	• May allow professionals to learn more about research • Potential for networking	• Expense
Training manual	• To support an active training process	• Helps to translate information into knowledge which can be applied	• Limited audience • Expense
Networking	• Associations of individuals / agencies which share a common goal or purpose and who contribute resources in two way exchange	• Reaches members who share common research interests. • Reduces 'reinventing of wheel' • Potential for interaction, discussion and review of findings	• Typically, low levels of active participation • Requires strong incentives for participation • Time consuming to operate and manage

Table 3. Dissemination pathways: comparison of relative advantages and disadvantages[1] (continued)

Method	Description	Advantages	Disadvantages
Internet, e-mail	• Worldwide electronic network of linked computers	• Immediate, convenient • Wide interest in electronic media	• Access to hardware limited in Southern countries • Potential may be, or is temporarily underdeveloped • Expense
Intermediaries	• Specialist agency intervening to disseminate and explain research to local constituency	• Ensures that research is translatable - based on local norms	• Problems may arise if research agenda of intermediaries is not consistent with research project
Popularisation, promotional artefacts	• As a means for reaching a wider audience. Influencing policy from below; uses mass media	• Reaches wide audience	• Core message may be diluted or misinterpreted during process of popularisation
Publicising	• Use of mass media as means of marketing new research	• Reaches wide audience at relatively low cost	• No control over interpretation of message
Participatory concept	• Knowledge disseminated to the community level using participatory techniques	• Translates research results into practical guidance at community level	• Time consuming
Policy briefs	• Directed at policy and decision makers	• Potential to influence on decision making process	• Difficulty in gaining access to decision makers
Interactive computer presentation	• Using PC software to demonstrate research findings	• High impact	• Difficulty in gaining access to decision makers • Limited access to hardware • Expense
Demonstrations	• Seeing research results on the ground can be persuasive	• High impact	• Limited audience

1. Adapted from Saywell and Cotton (1999) pp.56-7

Table 4. Methods for assessing the impact of dissemination pathways

Method	Comment
1. 'Bean counting' (records of requests; distribution figures) (NCDDR 1997; Haravu and Rajan 1996)	A basic form of tracking information. NCDDR promotes the use of electronic forms. The advantage is that all transactions can potentially be recorded. This method provides no insight into the use made of the information and its consequences (Health Information Forum 2000). Scott (1999) rejects the idea of taking dissemination measures such as these as a proxy measure of impact; they should at least be supplemented by additional methods (e.g. user opinions) to provide a valuable triangulation of data for evaluation (Glaser and Strauss 1968).
2. Recording web site hits (NCDDR 1997)	This is not a totally reliable method as a web site hit does not necessarily represent an incidence of use by a single user. It does, however, indicate increases and decreases in web site traffic.
3. Budget expenditure tracking (NCDDR 1997)	Impact may be reflected in savings made due to dissemination output. This may be in terms of time saved. Not all impacts can be easily quantified as a monetary value, for example, additional information may result in greater levels of skill and a higher quality output but may lead to no timesavings.
4. Citation analysis (Haravu and Rajan 1996)	There are strong arguments both for (Broadus, R.N. 1985; Kelland, J.L and Young, A.P. 1998) and against (Line, M.B. 1985; MacRoberts, M.H. and MacRoberts, B.R.1996) the use of citation frequencies as an indicator of document use or value.
5. Documentation of target audience changes (in press) (NCDDR 1997)	This relies on secondary sources and external agendas and interpretations of impact that may not address the main areas of concern.
6. Feedback cards included with materials (NCDDR 1997)	This method allows brief feedback. It relies on action by the receiver to return the card, therefore response rates are poor.
7. Follow up telephone calls (NCDDR 1997)	This is similar to feedback cards but action is instigated by the sender, so a higher level of response is expected. The depth of feedback varies depending on the nature of the survey.
8. Questionnaire to all recipients (Haravu and Rajan 1996)	This relies on action by the receiver to send back the card. Response rates are poor. Several versions of the questionnaire may be more useful than a single, generic version.
9. Secret ballot (Shaw and Jawo 1999)	The Stepping Stones Gambia programme used secret ballots to assess changes in behaviour and knowledge following an HIV awareness campaign. They found that respondents did not always understand that a negative response to a question could be correct and was permissible. These may be particularly useful if the nature of the information is sensitive or not usually discussed.

Table 4. Methods for assessing the impact of dissemination pathways *(continued)*

10. Structured questionnaires/interviews (Haravu and Rajan 1996)	A stratified sample should be used, recognising the country, subject and institution. Questions specific to specialist groups are required.
11. Unstructured interviews (Adams and Wood 1998; Haravu and Rajan 1996, (Shaw and Jawo 1999)	A stratified sample should be used, recognising the country, subject and institution. Access to rich, specific and anecdotal evidence is possible. Interviews are more likely than questionnaires to uncover criticisms.
12. Focus groups (NCDDR 1997, (Shaw and Jawo 1999)	These should comprise individuals who reflect the characteristics of the target audience. Access to rich, specific and anecdotal evidence is possible.
13. Case study analysis (Stephens, 1998)	Within this approach, a range of methods may be used such as focused interviews and policy document analysis.

References

DFID (1997) Eliminating World Poverty: A Challenge for the 21st Century. *White Paper on International Development*. DFID, London.

DFID (2001) *Meeting the Challenge of Poverty in Urban Areas: Strategies for Achieving the International Development Targets*. DFID, London.

Gosling, L. and Edwards, M. (1998) *Toolkits: a practical guide to assessment, monitoring, review and evaluation*. Development Manual 5. Save the Children, London.

Haravu, L.J. and Rajan, T.N. (1998) *Impact of semi-arid tropical crops information service (SATCRIS) at ICRISAT*. http://www.idrc.ca/en/ev-8958-201-1-DO-TOPIC.html (Accessed Nov 2003)

House of Commons Committee of Public Accounts (2003) *Department for International Development: maximising impact in the water sector*. DFID, London.

Menou, M.J. (2000) *Assessing methodologies in studies of the impact of information: a synthesis*. http://www.bellanet.org/partners/AISI/proj/synthesis.htm

NCDDR (1997) Dissemination evaluation strategies and options. *Research Exchange* 2 (2). http://www.ncddr.org/researchexchange/archives.html (Accessec Nov 2003)

Saywell, D.L. and Cotton, A.P. (1999) *Spreading the Word: Practical Guidelines for Research Dissemination Strategies*. WEDC, Loughborough, UK.

Saywell, D.L., Woodfield, J. and Cotton, A.P. (2000) *Dissemination pathways and indicators of impact and development*. WEDC, Loughborough, UK.

Schilderman, T. (2002) *Strengthening the knowledge and information systems of the urban poor*. ITDG, UK

Shaw, M. and Jawo, M. (1999) Gambian experiences with Stepping Stones: 1996-1999. *PLA Notes 37*. International Institute for Environment and Development. http://www..stratshope.org/ssgambia.html (Accessed Nov 2003)

Stephens, C. (1998) *Urban Environment, Poverty and Health: the influence of environmental health research on international and national urban policy elite.* Report of Research Activities and Results. London School of Hygiene and Tropical Medicine, London.

WEDC/ITAD (2002) *Evaluation of DFID's Research Dissemination.* WEDC, Loughborough, UK.

Woodfield, J. (2001) *Practice what you Preach: Phase One Impact Survey Analysis Report.* WEDC, Loughborough, UK.

World Bank (1998) World Development Report. World Bank: Washington, DC.

Printed in the USA
CPSIA information can be obtained
at www.ICGtesting.com
JSHW012046140824
68134JS00034B/3285